D0342267

LET EVENING COME

LET EVENING COME

REFLECTIONS
ON AGING

•

MARY C. MORRISON

PREFACE BY MORRIS L. WEST

DOUBLEDAY
New York • London • Toronto • Sydney • Auckland

PUBLISHED BY DOUBLEDAY

a division of Bantam Doubleday Dell Publishing Group, Inc.

1540 Broadway, New York, New York 10036

DOUBLEDAY and the portrayal of an anchor with a dolphin are

trademarks of Doubleday, a division of Bantam Doubleday

Dell Publishing Group, Inc.

Book design by Kathy Kikkert

Library of Congress Cataloging-in-Publication Data

Morrison, Mary Chase.

Let evening come: reflections on aging / by Mary C.

Morrison; preface by Morris L. West.—1st ed.

p.   cm.

1. Old age—Philosophy. 2. Aging—Psychological aspects.

3. Aging—Religious aspects. I. Title.

HQ1061.M63   1998

305.26′01—DC21   97-19578

CIP

ISBN 0-385-49086-0

February 1998

First Edition

1   3   5   7   9   10   8   6   4   2

To all the Old Ones of my youth,
who taught me that aging could have dignity.

And to all the Young,
who, now that I am old,
are teaching me in their turn
by the amazing generosity of their love.

LET EVENING COME

Let the light of late afternoon
shine through chinks in the barn, moving
up the bales as the sun moves down.

Let the cricket take up chafing
as a woman takes up her needles
and her yarn. Let evening come.

Let dew collect on the hoe abandoned
in long grass. Let the stars appear
and the moon disclose her silver horn.

Let the fox go back to its sandy den
Let the wind die down. Let the shed
go black inside. Let evening come.

To the bottle in the ditch, to the scoop
in the oats, to air in the lung
let evening come.

Let it come, as it will, and don't
be afraid. God does not leave us
comfortless, so let evening come.

—Jane Kenyon

PREFACE

This is a beautiful little book.

I have never met the woman who wrote it—because I live on the other side of the world. I cherish, however, a faint hope that one day before we both move off the planet, we may meet and touch hands and exchange a smile of recognition and understanding.

We both belong to the same generation. We have moved off the middle ground onto the high ridge from which we can see all the past spread below us and glimpse—on a clear day!—the shining towers of the kingdom which lies on the far side of the valley.

We have both faced the same questions and come up with much the same answers. To enjoy the inevitable process of aging, one does need the courage to be content—though never satisfied—to maintain a whole list of unfinished business, and to add to the list, new ventures every day. The stature of the self diminishes, the place it occupies in life gets narrower, but the spirit is liberated and flies in freer air.

The diminishments of age and its real afflictions are treated openly and courageously. The dependence we acknowledge frees us from the burden of trying to control others. We fear less, because the long tomorrow presents itself as a respite and a relief from the griefs of today. The love we can still give is unconditional. The love we receive is doubly precious.

I was happy as I read this testament of courageous capitulation.

Wise elders do not engage in combat; and all their victories are quiet ones.

—Morris L. West

LET EVENING COME

A standard complaint about writings on old age is that they are either too bright and determinedly cheerful, or too dark and gloomy. My hope in this small book is to bring the two extremes together without denying either one, for both are valid.

"Old age is not for the fainthearted." That saying has become almost a proverb; and it's true. Aging takes courage. To preside over the disintegration of one's own body, looking on as sight and hearing, strength, speed, and short-term memory deteriorate, calls for a heroism that is no less impressive for being quiet and patient. To watch the same process taking place in someone

whom one loves requires another kind of heroism, expressed in patience, devotion, and care. And to endure or watch the kind of deterioration that leaves, in the end, only the empty shell of a person, as with Alzheimer's, calls for a heroism in total defeat that is beyond words. Old age is not for the fainthearted, and anyone who watches it closely and with a sympathetic eye can sometimes be lost in admiration for the aging and their gallantry.

Where does this gallantry come from? How are we going to find it in ourselves, as we need it? What will this newfound present of old age and its unknown future, full of diminishments of all kinds, demand of us? Where is dignity to be found in it? How shall we find in ourselves the dignity that we see is needed?

This brings me to my second quotation. "Strength and energy fail as time moves on, but the spirit continues to produce great things," Marion Morris, a bacteriologist/immunologist, said in her eighties. The spirit—psyche—the soul—the self—the inner life: by whatever name, this is the area of life and growth and work for our old age.

Earlier in the same interview, Marion Morris said, "The more I live, the more I marvel at C. G. Jung's words: 'I do not live, but life is lived in me.' While I understand what Jung means when he says that we 'happen' to ourselves, I also follow his advice to watch what I do so I can find out who I am. This keeps me very busy."

The difficulties of old age give us the area—I could say the *arena*—in which we can take up this old-age challenge of finding out who we are. Dealing with these difficulties, we can grow in self-knowledge. We can even become wise. We can learn how to live into old age well, how to move on gracefully, how to go with the flow of life.

Let me tell a parable, in good biblical tradition. A certain young woman went one day to visit each of two elderly friends. Pressed for time, she could stay only fifteen minutes instead of the hour that she usually spent with each one. The first woman said, "Why did you bother to come at all if that's all the time you can spend with me?" The second woman said, "But it's so good of you to make the time for me when you are so busy." Now which of them do you think is headed into a happy day and a happy old age?

As our years go imperceptibly by, the difficulties of age catch up with us almost as imperceptibly. We begin to find more and more things to complain about, and do not notice at all how much we are complaining. We vaguely notice that people who come to see us seem impatient to get away, and do not notice at all how we are clutching at them and their time and their lives, like the Ancient Mariner holding his guests unwillingly riveted to the spot by his tale of endless sorrows. With more and more things to complain about, we never stop to notice that some are incidental, which we could and should change, if we put our minds to it, without further comment; while others are an inevitable part of

the aging process and should be lived with as simply and quietly as possible.

In order to learn who we are, we need to look at our attitudes: watch them day by day, notice how we approach life. More than ever, the old saying becomes true: it is not what happens to us but what we make of it that counts. This takes vigilance. An eighty-year-old cousin remarked to me once that at her age one had to be constantly alert not to be a bore to younger people. "You surely don't have any problem with that," I said. "You'd be surprised!" she replied fervently. She knew herself intimately, seeing what I, who looked on from the outside, could never see; and she knew the inner work that she must do to keep level with life as it moved her along into old age.

What inner tools do we need for this inner work?

First of all, if we have never done it before, we need to begin keeping a journal—not a diary of daily outward events, but a thoughtful writing-down of happenings, thoughts, dreams, nightmares, things we read or hear that seem important: whatever claims our attention for whatever reason. Most important, we need to write down thoughtfully our responses to them, both our immediate reaction and our later considerations. Nothing will make us aware of our attitudes as well as this exercise; nothing will help us as well to sort out what is important to us, and what of all our lifetime store of soul furniture we want to keep or discard. A journal is an instrument of awareness, through which we can watch what we do so we can find out who we are.

Second, we need to become comfortable with paradox—paradox, the collision of irreconcilable opposites that sparks light into a truth beyond either one. Paradox may have touched us only lightly, from time to time, in years past; now in old age it rules our lives. Failure is success. Loss is gain. Defeat is victory. Every loss contains a gift. Losing one's life is finding it. Find yourself. Lose yourself. In my end is my beginning. In my beginning is my end. Many of the great life truths come stated in paradox, and we have heard them often. Now in old age we begin to experience them.

Third, we must learn to live with continuing questions to which there seem to be no immediate answers. This was always the case, but in the speed and busyness of younger life we hardly noticed it. What has life been, in all its stages? What is it now? What will death be? Who and what are we? Now these questions rise up before us. At no time in our life process is Rilke's instruction more relevant than it is now—to love the questions and live along into the answers. And those questions all come down to one personal, intimate one: how are we going to respond to the inevitable and growing diminishment that is coming upon us?

So let us love that question, and begin.
One step at a time. Perhaps the first step comes
when we suddenly realize that we have moved up
a generation and are now no longer the younger
generation—we learned that some years ago,
without too much pain—or even the middle one.
For some of us it happens on the job as we see
other, younger people beginning to take over the
work that for so long we have done well and
considered ours. For others, as it did with me, it
happens within the family context.

JOURNAL ENTRY, AUGUST 29, 1978

After a four-year lapse in visiting the Florida home
and family, I found one thing deeply and
disturbingly different this spring. Maxey and I were
now the oldest generation. No more middle ground
for us. Our children and nephews and nieces were
occupying that spot. Our parents, uncles, and aunts
had either died or moved into retirement centers of
one sort or another. And now we were in the time
slot marked "Old."

> *Regardons l'album de photographie:*
> *Les jeunes sont vieux;*
> *Les vieux sont morts.*
> *—Tournons la page.*

> *Let's look at the photograph album:*
> *The young are old;*
> *The old are dead.*
> *—Let's turn the page.*

Yes indeed. And this is one of those phenomena of life that outwardly seem ordinary and human and simple but are inwardly complex and convoluted. It was difficult to adjust to it—difficult, even, to find out where the pressure points of the inward discomfort were. The best way of describing the most immediate and central one is this:

We were no longer where the action was. We were no longer where the decisions, large and small, were being made. We were out on the sidelines; we had been called out of the game. A bad feeling/a good feeling, it was some of both—but definitely a strange feeling, and a new relationship to the family, both immediate and extended.

We were included in things—eating, sailing, beaching especially—and fortunately we are spry and can take an easy and natural part in it all. But for

the rest, it was a matter of seeing busy people make time for us, and usually time that was hard to make. And of course this will get more so when, as, if we get less able to be active. The other day I said something to my stepmother about making a trip to Florida to see the gang, and she said, "How would I see them? I can't do those hours at the beach; I don't like sailing; I can't fly around at top speed the way they do. So why go?" I remember too my favorite older-generation cousin saying, when I used to go to see her, "You're the only person who doesn't talk to me as if I were an old lady."

Throughout life the relative positions change; and no one has put much time into thinking through this last change, the process of becoming the oldest generation. I remember vividly the moment when the then middle generation, uncles, aunts, parents, began to receive me into the Glorious Company of Adults. The crossing over was clearly delineated, with a well-marked road ahead. This new road is not marked at all, and I am feeling its uncertainties strongly. The uncertainties, the restrictions, the opportunities trail off into a whole perspective of question marks losing themselves in the distance and over the hill.

Do we detach ourselves and make a new life? With our family job done, do we move on? And to what? Do we still consider ourselves part of the family whole? What whole? And what part?

If we live along into these questions some answers begin to emerge. Do we detach ourselves? Yes, decidedly. It is time to give up the old habit of being in control, of deciding what is to be done or not done. This is difficult. We have spent the best years of our lives learning the managerial skills that family life demands, to a point where they have become second nature. How can we possibly lay them down? But now we must do so, and as gracefully as possible.

The facts are there, if we will look at them. We no longer need to know exactly what is going on at every moment. We no longer need to orchestrate the days as they go by. We are no longer responsible for the quality of life within the family or the group. Other people are doing that now, and it should comfort us that some of them, at least, are the very people we have had a chance to influence and guide, in whom we can and should place our confidence. Or if not—well, it is out of our hands, and we need to recognize that fact. And actually, once looked at in this way, is it not a great relief? We need—no, now we are free!—to move quietly out of the center of family life and into its circumference.

Do we still consider ourselves part of the family whole? Yes, of course. And what part? Well—it is almost a platitude that grandparents and grandchildren get along together more harmoniously than parents and children, and with luck and good management we may begin to explore the truth of that. Our grandchildren look to us for comfort and unconditional love when they are small; and we can give it because we are not responsible for them. We can see them for what they are because we are not guilt-ridden by what we think they ought to be. We can savor their growth because we have the perspective to see how fleeting childhood is; when we were parents, living with it day by day, it seemed to go on forever. We can befriend their adolescence because of the more relaxed attitude toward conventions and outward demands that we have acquired (if we have managed to acquire it, that is). We may even find them turning to us for

some of our old-fashioned thoughts, the ones
that we have found basic over the years, to guide
them. We can provide a "haven of peace and rest"
for them, and perhaps for our children too,
caught up as they are in the responsibilities of
middle life.

A marvelous, warm place waits for us on
the periphery of family life; all that it asks of us is
to live along gently into it, aware of its promises
and possibilities.

Here, too can come an early illustration of the old-age paradox, "Loss is gain." For now we are free—with a freedom that perhaps we hardly know how to use—to explore a new set of possible relationships, based on interests and personal tastes rather than blood ties. Now is the time par excellence for rediscovering friendship as a priority in our lives, for making new friends and reconnecting in a new way with old ones. Now is the time for painting classes, hiking clubs, bird watching, Elderhostel, volunteering for work that is of interest; not merely to keep busy but to meet new friends, older and younger. Now is our chance to savor one of life's greatest pleasures, that of working on a common interest with congenial friends.

All this may require an examination of what I have come to call the Noah's Ark syndrome, the idea that two people pair off and from then on never do anything separately. Those outside this pairing system—widows, widowers, single people—can speak feelingly of how restrictive it is, how pervasively, unconsciously, and monotonously it structures all areas of life. Now is the time for married couples to become aware of how it restricts them too. Perhaps our togetherness habits need some reexamination; perhaps fifty years, or thereabouts, is long enough to refer all our interests and tastes to those of another person, however close, however beloved. We can open

up the possibility that by developing different areas of interest, even different friends, we will bring new things home to share, and so greatly enlarge our lives together.

T. S. Eliot says that the old ought to be explorers. It may be a new thought that in old age the nature of our relationships can and should be explored. If so, it is a new thought that needs thinking, for it will greatly enlarge our lives.

A second life step comes when we stand in front of a mirror or look at an all-too-candid camera shot and realize to the full that by no stretch of the imagination could the word "young" ever be applied to us again, or even the term "middle aged." We are old. For me this moment came when I looked at a photograph someone had snapped of me as I took a nap; the legs curled up on the sofa were unmistakably the thin shanks of an old woman—not even a young-old woman, an old-old woman. "I am an old woman," I heard myself saying aloud. It was my first experience of that particular truth.

What to do? First, mourn, of course. Youth, middle age have now become old age; what can we do but mourn those thin shanks and all that they stand for? The losses are many. Strength, easy energy, vigor, elasticity, muscle tone, skin tone, conventional beauty. A whole world is gone; no wonder we mourn. Our task now is to keep mourning from turning into

envy—envy of those who are still young, envy of that whole world of life that once we knew. But if we can get beyond that, perhaps we can begin to move into the rugged acceptance exemplified by Chaucer's sturdy Wife of Bath:

> *Whan that it remembereth me*
> *Upon my yowthe, and on my jolitee,*
> *It tikleth me aboute myn herte roote,*
> *Unto this day it doth myn herte boote*
> *That I have had my world as in my tyme.*
> *But age, allas! that al wol envenyme,*
> *Hath me biraft my beautee and my pith;*
> *Lat go, fare-wel, the devel go therewith!*

Once we have managed to say, "Let go, farewell," it becomes possible to step back a few lines into the poem and realize that yes, indeed, it does our hearts good to think that we have had our world as in our time. For we have, you know. It was our time and we lived it. It happened and therefore it exists. It exists in our hearts and memories, and no one can take it from us. There is "A time for the evening under lamplight/ (The evening with the photograph album)," T. S. Eliot says, and this is it. People often deplore the tendency of the old to live in the past; and sometimes it *is* deplorable. But even then it is the shadow half of a process that can be very good, and one that this period of our lives requires of us—the "harvesting" of our past in memory, in thought, in writing. Each of us has at least one volume of memoirs stored away in our minds and hearts. It is time to look at the whole in perspective and garner its wisdom.

Our memories can also be a treasure trove for our children and younger friends. One old man, beginning to write his memoirs, found that as his short-term memory began to fail his long-term memory was raising up for him childhood events he had not thought of since they happened. In the end he produced, in several chapters of total recall, a priceless documentary of life in a small New England college town in the 1880s and '90s. His son, urged in old age to follow his father's example, protested that he had nothing interesting to write about—and proceeded to produce three volumes containing, among other good things, a pair of chapters on life as a boy on a decaying James River plantation in the second decade of this century.

The treasure that this harvesting can be for oncoming generations is nothing to the treasure that it can be for us. We have had our world as in our time, and if we relive it well in memory, it will bring us wisdom. We will come, each of us, to see our life as the whole that it is. Events that seemed random will show themselves to be parts of a coherent whole. Decisions that we were hardly aware of making will reveal themselves as significant choices, and we can honestly and dispassionately regret the poor ones and rejoice in the good ones. We can call up emotions that seemed devastating in their time, and recollect them in tranquillity, forgiving others and ourselves. When we do this we have truly had our world as in our time, and it is in our possession from that time on, giving us its gifts of wisdom and wholeness.

Now we can look with new eyes at the present, and at those younger ones who are having their world in their time. Now, if our hearts are in the right place, if we have done our harvesting well, we can look at them and love them in their passage through the stages that we remember well, but are now seeing from a different perspective, as beautiful parts of a whole that we could not see while we were living it.

JOURNAL ENTRY, DECEMBER 31, 1990

One of the high points—the highest, in fact, of Christmastime for me this year was a visit from The Young.

I was putting cookie dough on a cookie sheet and happened to look up out of the window, and there they were, coming along the walkway, talking and laughing, full of the excitement generated among people who are fond of one another and are meeting for the first time in a good while. Lesa, Suzi, Tim: 27, 24, 23, youth in its most glorious maturity, with some choices made but all the possibilities of the future still ahead. Youth still close to that peak of physical beauty that it reaches in the late teens. Youth with plenty of problems to meet and decisions to make, but (perhaps because of the season) a pervading aura of peace, however temporary. Youth, above all, full of life, "the precious uncertain fire of life" burning without thought, unselfconscious, and so unconscious of its own beauty, a fine clear blaze.

"*J'aime la jeunesse* [I love youth]," Olga Lamkert used to say when she was about as old as I am now; and I used to be put off by the impersonality of the phrase. But yes, it's true. What was coming along the walk toward me was beyond personality: a gift that its owners were unaware of, or if they thought about it at all, thought of as part of themselves, not as the temporary loan that it is. "We do not live life; life lives us." Childhood lives us; maturity lives us; old age lives us. And I, in old age, can say with Olga, "*J'aime la jeunesse.*" And I particularly love it when it lives in people who are using it well, as these three are.

Somebody (Bernard Shaw?) once said that youth is wasted on the young. It's true in more senses than he may have intended: wasted because misused; wasted because not appreciated as the gift of health, strength, and energy that it is; but also wasted because the young are unaware of the clear beauty that is theirs for the time.

Perhaps it is only the old, looking on, who can see that beauty. Perhaps that is one of the gifts of old age.

But these chances to enjoy the beauty of youth depend greatly upon whether or not the young enjoy being with us. If they do, all we have to do is *be* there; they will come as often as they can. They will invite themselves for visits; it will be difficult to keep them away. For their own lovely and mysterious reasons, the young—some of them at least—are eager to treasure and wonder at the old people in their lives.

What are the elders like whom they seek out? First of all they are people who seem to feel at home with themselves and with the world around them. They seem to have a life of their own, either in action or simply in *being*; they are glad to see visitors but seem to have no desperate

need of them, or of any other distraction. They are people who have become complete in themselves in some enviable, hard-to-grasp way.

They still keep track of the world and care a great deal about what happens in it. One old woman I know gained fame among her younger relatives because they knew they would have to read the *New York Times* the morning before they went to see her, if they wanted to keep up their end of the conversation. She would want to know what they thought about all the new and interesting things that were happening in the world. She did a crossword puzzle daily, in much the same mood as an athletic person might go to a fitness center. One old man drew the young by being dramatically and even flamboyantly himself—a true original, whom it was great fun just to watch in action.

These easy-to-visit elders are more interested in the lives of their visitors than in their own. They want to hear what the young are doing and reading and thinking. They are apt to dwell not on problems but on what life offers that is promising and lively. There is a refreshing agility in their thinking. In their opinions they seem almost to have graduated from morality, as it were, and to look at each situation that is presented to them on its own individual merits, freshly, not stretched on any Procrustes' bed of preconceptions, but seen in the light of its own integrity and that of the person presenting it.

Above all they offer peace and perspective, and a warm and welcoming place that the young find restful, and that they come to

seek, as one would seek a lost and legendary treasure. One old woman cautioned a grandson who had asked to come for a visit, "Don't expect any action. All I have to offer is a cozy time by the fire." To which he replied, "Don't underestimate *cozy!*"

This is a daunting picture. Who can be such a person as that? Where do we begin? An encouraging fact is that life helps us along the way. We are engaged in a natural process which, if we let it, will bring us out in this good place. As the old parable says, the seed knows what to do: "first the blade, then the ear, then the full grain in the ear." The first half of life insists that we develop a good, energetic, driving ego that will enable us to do what we need to do in the world—learn, work, establish a household, be a citizen. But somewhere along in the second half, a different voice begins speaking inside us.

JOURNAL ENTRY, JUNE 27, 1989

"Agis quod age [Do what you do]." Latin possibly faulty, but English not, except that I might want to put in an alternative reading: "Do what you are doing." Why do I keep forgetting that? Why do I keep looking ahead, looking back, looking in the mirror—at success, at failure, in short, wanting to be a *me,* an *I,* an active ego all the time?

Surely old age is the time, of all the life stages, when one can move into the pure happiness of being a nothing, a quiet center, not a *me* at all except as circumstances call forth the kind of action that needs a *me* to do it. And after that action, silence again, and freedom from the clamoring *me* that wants to be at the center of things, to be successful and admired and "popular and very truly run after," like Old Man Kangaroo in the *Just So Stories.* Perhaps, when I really look at the problem, what I need is not to be a nothing but to be a different kind of *me.*

Long years ago, in one of the very early Bible Study Groups, when we were looking at the

saying, "Unless you change and become like children, you will never enter the kingdom of heaven," we asked ourselves what children are like, really. It was a big question, because children are lots of things, not all of them necessarily pleasant or "good." Finally one of the group said, "A child's ego isn't self-regarding and self-seeking, like ours; it's just something she gets around with, does things with, looks at things with—a tool, really." We all suddenly felt sure that that was exactly what Jesus was talking about; and we were, for the moment at least, filled with a longing to be like that.

Now in old age I need that longing all the time. When I have it, I am happy; when I forget it, I am lost in all the diminishments and frustrations of old age, which make it impossible for me to be a *me* except in querulous and negative ways.

As we age, the old, driving ego becomes increasingly a bore to others and, more importantly, to ourselves. At this point we meet another one of old age's paradoxes: lose yourself; find yourself. Pay attention to what you do so you can find out who you are; and try to say goodbye to the old self that wants to make the world meet its demands. For those who will do this work, a new way of being, a new *"me,"* is accessible, and available—one that becomes at home in the world, and more and more the old, lost *me* of childhood.

One of childhood's outstanding characteristics is curiosity—endless curiosity about anything and everything. In old age we can reclaim curiosity. Conditioned in childhood by that recurrent adult admonition, "Don't be so nosy!" we grew up thinking of curiosity as a bad thing—an impression often confirmed by our own adult experiences of curiosity used as a tool for self-advancement or power, or the sheer pleasure of gossip. Now in old age curiosity can become innocent again, as it was in childhood, and serve, simply and without designs of any

kind, our outgoing interest in our surroundings.
We can look at the world and the people around
us with wonder and pleasure; and marvel, as
Miranda did in *The Tempest*, "O brave new
world/That has such people in't!" With nothing to
gain or lose, from hope and fear set free, we find
that we have new eyes if we will only lose old
habits, take up new ones, and become curiouser
and curiouser. We have been granted, before we
leave this world, a chance to look   really look—
at it, and see it freshly.

A third life step comes when we begin to notice that, as we age, strength and speed slacken off. Athletes find that their legs, arms, and general coordination will not do what they once did. The rest of us realize that it takes longer to do the daily tasks—dressing in the morning, eating meals, keeping house and yard orderly, everything we do, in fact. The easy agility of youth is gone. These are real losses, great losses.

JOURNAL ENTRY, OCTOBER 26, 1995

As a write-in-class assignment for the Journaling class that Barb Parsons and I are teaching at Pendle Hill this year, we were all to write about a physical piece of work that we did that day. And I wrote:

OK, so I got out of bed today. I opened one eye—my half-blind eye, for some reason, will open more willingly than the other one, and sometimes I have to push the other lid up. I looked around the room for a while, checking how much I could see today—some days are better than others. The painting of the boats in the bay, in the past so full of light, was black; so it was clearly not one of the better days.

I checked myself out here and there. It was not going to be one of those days when I want to make my bed and lie down on it immediately. So far, so good. Apart from one sore elbow, arms and legs seemed functional, so I sat up and threw the covers back, fortunately not sending flying the little

earphone radio that I take to bed with me in case I'm awake a long time in the night.

I stood up, but fell back on the bed again—it always takes two tries—stood up again, and took a few uncertain steps into the bathroom. At eighty-five it takes awhile to regain the upright posture which we learned at age one. There I looked into my bleary face in the mirror—and I wish I had remembered to say, as I sometimes do, what the old man in *The Milagro Beanfield War* said as he staggered to his washbasin and looked into his mirror— "Thank you, God, for another day."

Underlying this slowing-down process is a general loss of energy, a basic life fatigue, hardly noticeable at times, overpowering at other times, but always there. This tiredness brings its own gift if we are alert to discern it—another of the gifts of old age.

JOURNAL ENTRY, JUNE 19, 1990

As a result of past years and recent illnesses, we found ourselves tired and old this June in Vermont, sitting on benches a lot. At the other end of the scale, however, we found ourselves enjoying the clouds, the lake, the hills, the spring flowers, as perhaps never before.

It reminded me of an old uncle of mine, with hardly two brain cells left to flash signals to each other. He was taking his slow morning walk, and I, taking a brisker sixty-four-year-old walk, came upon him standing transfixed before a yucca in full bloom. When I touched his arm, he started, looked at me, pointed at the yucca, and said, "Look! How beautiful!"

When we used to climb mountains long ago, I always arrived at the top completely exhausted. I would lie down on a rock shelf looking out at the wide view, able to enjoy its beauty with an intensity

that I can't remember experiencing at any other time. I used to ask myself how much this ecstasy had to do with the fatigue that had laid me flat on the rock.

Now in age I feel that the two were connected. Now I think that this combination of exhaustion and ecstasy is one of the gifts of old age, almost exactly analogous to the mountain-climbing experience. We've been climbing for a long lifetime, pausing for rests, with good views along the way. Now there is no more climbing to do, and if there were, we couldn't do it because we are too tired. But the view is there; and we are exhausted enough to reach into (or be reached by) our ecstasy in it, all of it: water, skies, clouds, trees, flowers, mountains, people.

Look! How beautiful!

Our diminishing physical powers can open our minds to other insights, some of them a little on the wry side, but welcome just the same—if we will condescend to welcome them, that is. As for instance:

JOURNAL ENTRY, APRIL 24, 1994

In old age, great satisfaction comes from what to younger eyes may seem a very small achievement. Balance in walking, for instance; or simply seeing, however poorly. This week, for me, a great achievement—renewing my driver's license. Nothing to it at forty or fifty or sixty. But now, at eighty-four? Would the doctor clear me, medically? More important, could I pass the eye exam? Where is the local photograph station? Phone calls to police produced only press-the-button replies that answered none of my questions. And even if I found the place, would I get another photograph like the current one, which looked as if I had been carried in from the morgue to have it taken? In the end I passed the exams—found the photograph station— got a reasonably recognizable photograph—and felt as if I had won the marathon.

A mile walk can give me the same glow of achievement that a five-mile one used to bring. I can feel like Jack Horner when something comes up

easily and naturally from memory. If I manage to learn something new, I glow with a pleasure that life seldom gave me in youth, when I took all this for granted. There is nothing like old age to make one aware of the marvels of the human body and mind.

What is sight? I ask myself—and as my physical sight ebbs, I know seeing, simply seeing, for a marvel; and a kind of retroactive thanksgiving comes for the use, all those years, of that great gift. As our senses dim, seeing, hearing, walking, touching, tasting all reveal themselves to us at last as the miracles that they have always been.

Our mental processes slow down too. It takes longer to remember things, a slowness that we tend to identify anxiously as the beginning of the end. But if we will wait, the memory that we want—a name, a place, an event—will come to mind, swimming slowly to the surface of our minds, like a fish rising. Perhaps we can be as relaxed about it as the elderly Quaker who said, whenever he forgot something, "The Lord has taken it from me." If it comes, well; if not, perhaps it does not matter very much. Personality, character, and even the basic wisdom that life has brought can last far, far into the mental slowness and even confusion of old age.

As I was heading into late middle age my father reached a state in which he was never quite sure whether I was his sister or his daughter; I wish I had been wise enough then to realize how little importance that had. He was still his interested, interesting, and eternally curious self, and the wisdom of his years was still available—if only I had not been distracted by this minor, trivial mix-up. If only I had been agile enough to help him quickly past those tangled areas of his mind to ones where his mind could still move freely and well, I might have learned a great deal from him that is now lost.

For these areas exist, and can still be found. One old man I have known, who could hardly summon up enough of his short-term memory to remember the names of his grandchildren or understand a simple instruction, could still call upon all his lifelong love of nature to find his way around his familiar woods and identify the birds he saw, and hear their characteristic songs. What we have loved will stay with us still, often for a long, long time, even if other memories and knowledge forsake us.

The greatest challenge of old age may be the aloneness that comes as children leave home, friends move away, or longtime companions die who have shared our lives for many years. This last especially can feel as if life itself has been cut off; as indeed it has, the life that we have known and come to feel at home in. We hardly recognize ourselves in this new inner setting; it is as if we too have gone away somewhere, who knows where? It is almost like the old New England greeting: "How do you find yourself today?" and the wry answer: "I don't know—I'm still looking." We don't know, and we hardly know where to begin looking.

But here again is a gift waiting to be received. Now, in great hardship and deprivation, we are given the chance (as Henri Nouwen puts it) to "move from loneliness to solitude." In all our lives, probably, we have not taken time to be by ourselves, to *be* ourselves—to discover what our own individual tempo of living will turn out to be if left to itself; to learn what we think, how we feel, how we operate in a space—interior and exterior—that is wholly our own.

Now, in all the grief and pain of loneliness, we can turn from our long life of attending to others and begin to attend to ourselves—from feeling a great emptiness at the center to finding the riches of our own being that lie there waiting to be mined. We may come to love being alone, with time to befriend ourselves and find companionship in our own thoughts and feelings. In old age we may find solitude itself our best friend, our longtime companion; and we may be grateful, in the end, for this most challenging opportunity to find our own center, and to cherish what we find.

Solitude—it's not a word in everyday use, or in everyday thought. Newly arrived at a retirement center, a woman was asked to tell a group of other newcomers what her chief interests were; and when she said, "Silence and solitude," a dreadful silence descended, the kind that makes the person making it feel crude and out of place. We have no place for solitude in our culture; it is a word without a concept, a concept with no content. For some people solitude may have been a longing without a name for most of their lives.

JOURNAL ENTRY, JANUARY 25, 1997

In the Dolly Copp State Park in New Hampshire is a sign commemorating Dolly Copp, a farm wife of the past century who dissolved her marriage after fifty years with the comment, "Hayes is very well, but fifty years is long enough to be married." Most people who hear this story express the opinion that it must not have been much of a marriage if she would take such a drastic step in order to get rid of her husband. On the other hand, I tend to see nothing personal at all in her decision (after all, didn't she say, "Hayes is very well?") but only a desperate plea for time and space in which to find her own individual life, before it ended.

Some people are born loners, and I think I must be one of them. When I was a baby, Mama once told me, they would put me to bed at the usual baby hour and would come upstairs hours later to find me in my crib, wide awake, quiet, perfectly happy. In college I was always finding myself somehow alone in whatever I was doing. I

considered it a defect in my character and tried to overcome it, but with no success. In the family-raising time of my life, I managed to become pretty well socialized, though at stressful times the phrase from Psalms would come to mind, "He [God] setteth the solitary in families," and I would wonder if that was meant to be a promise or a threat.

Then, at the empty-nest turning point of middle age, something arose in me, and my journal became full of entries about being alone. I would write a long entry, and ten years later another; and then I would come upon the first by accident, discovering with astonishment that the two entries were almost identical. I had not yet learned to dignify it with the name of Solitude, but I knew what I wanted, what I needed—as if my life was depriving me of something as essential as the air I breathed.

Solitude does not arise out of loneliness automatically, however, even for those who consciously seek it.

JOURNAL ENTRY, SEPTEMBER 19, 1981

So now I am having what I keep longing for—a time alone in the cabin without any sense of shirking my responsibilities, as Maxey is away on a hiking trip.

But time alone is not easy, even when you have longed for it and been given a free gift of it. Being alone makes me realize what a poor naked wretch I am (I've been rereading *King Lear* and it shows), what a basic emptiness I am, how it takes all the resources of the outward world to keep me going—books, radio, the fire in the fireplace, food, letters in the mailbox. And I wish I had the courage and the endurance simply to stay completely empty and see what comes to me out of the emptiness. And it feels as if most of the sins and crimes of the human race have risen out of desperately trying to cover that nakedness and avoid that emptiness.

Well—but then there is some ecstasy too, when something does fill the emptiness, when all

your surroundings speak to you in love; the sun
really shines, the rain really falls; when you are tired
or sick and you feel yourself picked up and carried
somehow.

Time alone in the dark and the light—worth
it both ways.

Whether we seek it or have it forced on us, this kind of time alone (that is first of all loneliness before it can become solitude) leads us to look at time itself.

JOURNAL ENTRY, OCTOBER 17, 1995

Where has time gone? When I was growing up, seventy years ago, there was plenty of time, the best sort of time. Time to goof off, to do nothing, and simply grow. Even in my children's growing-up days they had that kind of time, at least in the summers, to lie in hammocks and read and think and just grow.

The need to grow doesn't stop, even in old age; and I think I do some of my best growing when I'm lying in bed in the morning, slowly getting my eyes open.

I wonder if the interest in meditation these days is not perhaps an attempt to find this lost and legendary treasure, time. Of course in the Eastern cultures, it is usually billed as timelessness; but for us Westerners, I think it is really time that we are

looking for. I wonder if it vanished when digital watches came in, presenting, as they do, one isolated second vanishing into another endlessly—in contrast to clock faces, which show time visually as a waiting space. I am coming to have a real sense of time as the fourth dimension, a lost aspect of the space in which a truly human life is lived.

In old age we can begin to acquire a new
sense of time, not as rushing past us, demanding
that we run to keep up with it, but as a significant
emptiness, waiting for us to live in it and fill it
with thought and feeling, a constantly present
now, like the tone of a bell:

> *A bell says Now Now Now*
> *tells in one syllable the news—*
> *in single drops*
> *with circling rings of echoes*
>   *round each one.*
> *As one note dies*
> *and consciousness begins to drift away,*
> *the bell repeats and calls us back*
> *to presence and the moment and the now.*

Left to ourselves, we can never stay with the now. Our minds keep drifting off to past or future, and for the most part we live in a dream, ignoring the present moment, which is the only reality we have. It is one of the coping mechanisms that life has taught us; but now we need to unlearn it.

Some people, in moments of crisis and great need, have made the discovery that simple attention to the present—"Now I am breathing in; now I am breathing out; now I am walking to the doorway; here is the sunshine, and the breeze feels fresh on my skin"—will steady them momentarily, or even get them through days and weeks of a difficult period. In these moments of attention to the present, each moment stands alone and becomes a visitation, a presence in its own right.

For, when we pay attention to the present moment, suddenly it is no longer squeezed to nothing between past and future. Suddenly we can stand still in it, no longer running desperately past one moment into the next, like a caged squirrel on its exercise wheel. We find ourselves in a divine moment; and the divine moment is now, the Eternal Now. Any moment, every moment can give us its full presence—and its present of an inner space for new light and fresh insight.

In this new state we have time, plenty of
time, for noticing details—shade and light and
color in nature, in the characters of people
around us, in the weather of our own hearts.
"Time is but the stream I go a-fishing in," Thoreau
said; and like him, we too can savor the full flavor
of things as they happen, finding in each moment
riches that we never knew existed. All this we can
now do in the simplicity of childhood, but with
the full consciousness and ripeness of memory
that a long life brings. It is amazing how much
rich experience time will bring us when we move
through it slowly in this way.

We may find that in living this new life of
silence and slow time we are giving a gift not
only to ourselves but to others as well. One old
woman apologized to a pair of younger weekend

visitors for the snail's pace at which she lived her days, only to have them make the apparently heartfelt statement, "We *like* your pace."

Situations and attitudes come to look different now that time itself is different. For instance, waiting:

JOURNAL ENTRY, JANUARY 13, 1994

How the whole quality of waiting changes in old age! For me in youth it was a strip of impatience between two events. Now in age it has become an action in itself, one that I find myself strangely ready, even happy, to engage in. As Elsie Anderson said to me one day in her nineties, after eighty-five years of brisk and almost incessant activity: "Who would ever have thought that I would be perfectly happy, as I am, just sitting here looking out of the window at the seasons as they come and go?" But she could—and I can. I can sit, on a station bench, or in a doctor's office, or anywhere, and wait, almost like the mysterious figure in George Fox's dream, "looking at time how it passed away," and attend either to what is going on around me, or to my own thoughts, or to a strange, patiently expectant inner stillness that I haven't found words to describe. Mysteriously, waiting has acquired its own identity,

its own value, and brings its own reward. I don't understand that, but there it is.

When old age took from George Macdonald (the nineteenth-century preacher and writer, author of such childhood classics as *The Princess and the Goblin*) his intellectual powers and left him in a state of great simplicity, he spent his days waiting, simply waiting. He would sit all day in a room with his eyes fixed on the doorway. No one knew whom he expected; but as time went on the people close to him began to surmise that it was no one of this world. When someone appeared in the doorway, his face would light up; but it was never the expected one, and he would settle back again, without impatience, to his waiting. Reading this story in my thirties, I found it pathetic. Not anymore. Waiting has become a quality of being, a reality that I sometimes live in, and would like to understand better, for it can bring me great things.

The new sense of time brings in, for those of us who love to read, a new way of reading. Through all our busy years we learned to read with purpose—to pass an exam, to prepare for an interview, to carry our share of a social conversation, to keep up with what is going on in the world. Or we learned to read for distraction—"distracted from distraction by distraction," as Eliot puts it—in order to take our minds off our problems for an hour or two. Now at last we can reclaim reading, real reading, and move back to those long-gone days in the hammock, when we were reading for sheer enjoyment, and for the pleasure of living in other worlds of experience not ours, or not yet ours.

Surprisingly, we find a great change taking place in the kind of thing we want to read. Poetry—how long is it since we seriously read poetry? Yet long-forgotten lines rise up in memory, and we turn back to them, finding that

the poems in which they are embedded resonate
with our present experience in ways that we
never could have imagined at that long-ago first
reading. Tennyson—who reads Tennyson
nowadays? Yet we turn back to him now, and we
find him saying:

> *Though much is taken, much abides; and though*
> *We are not now that strength which in old days*
> *Moved earth and heaven; that which we are, we are.*

Yes, indeed. And Shakespeare—we haven't read any of his plays since college. Yet King Lear and Polonius come to mind, and we begin rereading, seeing with the new eyes of age the astonishing depth and richness of imagination that created these incredible combinations of folly and wisdom—incredible, that is, until we are startled by finding them hidden within our own aging process. One of Jane Austen's best comic creations, Mr. Woodhouse, in *Emma*, presents all that anyone needs in the way of a cautionary tale about the gentle, demanding selfishness that the weaknesses of old age can tempt us to sink into. As someone once remarked, "A sweet little old lady can easily keep six people fully occupied in taking care of her."

Other gifts lie hidden in the pages of history, biography, novels, poems, and plays, in which the great writers bring their wisdom to cast light on the whole scope of our experience and the whole sweep of history, to give us the perspective and wisdom that we need to guide us in our looking back, our looking forward, and our now. Painters and sculptors put things into perspective too; anyone who really looks at Rembrandt's series of self-portraits or Rodin's statue of an aging woman can hardly come away from the experience unchanged.

"These fragments I have shored against my ruins," T. S. Eliot said of significant passages from his reading. In age we have—are?—ruins, and need all the shoring up we can get; and here it is, in the insights and imaginations of life as understood by the geniuses of human history.

Miracles that they are, where do they come from? Do they by any chance come from any source that is open to us?

JOURNAL ENTRY, SEPTEMBER 11, 1992

I was talking the other day about Pop to Steve, his grandson and namesake, saying that he was the only person I have ever known personally who seemed to me to be a genius—not because he was outstanding, but because of the way his mind worked. His creative ideas—and he had many—seemed to rush into his mind all at once on their own initiative, the way Mozart "heard" his music.

Vivid dreams are another way such insights and inspirations come—though that's not another way, really, but just the same way in sleep. I've thought for a long time that these vivid dreams are where poetry comes from. Several dream-events (of being a bag lady with nowhere to lay my head, for instance, or of being able to run freely without getting out of breath) have brought me to think that one function, at least, of dreams is to extend our experience, to give us limited human beings a wider

range of experience and insight than we would ever be able to come at in "real" life. It's even possible— likely—that we experience them (beautiful, terrifying, whatever) more intensely than we could in real life.

And we wake up, and there, left over from the dream, is a whole area of experience to write down and live into and reflect on, and understand, and incorporate into our life.

I think that this process is where
Shakespeare's incredible range of experience came
from. Hamlet, Ophelia, Othello, Desdemona, Lady
Macbeth, Iago, Falstaff, Henry V—how did he
know them? (Let alone a whole host of middle-range
and minor characters.) And if you ever find yourself
in the middle of an experience like that of any of
them, you know firsthand that Shakespeare is right
on target. How does he do it?

Only through dreams, I think—dreams lived
with and into, dreams supplementing life, deepening
life. The Dream as Art, I've called it before. Other
people exemplify the same process to me—Blake, of
course, and Coleridge. The two Brontës, Emily and
Charlotte—where did they get their wildness? And
Tolstoy at times—how did he ever come at the
inwardness of being a prisoner on the long French
retreat from Moscow? To take it further, where do
painters and sculptors learn to see? Where does the
music come from that composers hear in their
inward ears and write down?

Dreams are an extreme, pure-gift form of

imagination, benevolent and terrifying. They come, offering me an experience of insanity in a form that needs no living out, or at the other extreme an experience of beatific states that I have not earned. They give me vivid mental pictures; they solve—by an intuitive rising above them—problems that my conscious mind cannot solve. They are where wisdom and poetry come from, and perhaps all creativity, whether we realize it or not.

We too, in our own small way, can tap into this creative resource by paying attention to our most vivid dreams, terrifying or benign—*The Dream as Art*—recording them in our journals, "befriending" them by visiting them from time to time in thought and writing, trying by every means in our power to capture every aspect of what they mean to us and are trying to teach us. We can be artists in the understanding of our own lives.

Solitude, silence, and slow time have other gifts to give us.

JOURNAL ENTRY, JULY 28, 1978

Time for another summing up, which perhaps I can best do by describing yesterday evening. Helen and Maxey had gone down to get Helen's car, which had been repaired at Racine's. I was sitting at the table, looking out over the lake in the intervals of working at some calligraphy, when, suddenly, there came something. It was like a voice, like an embrace, like someone coming up behind me and laying two hands on my shoulders. And what the whole experience, which surrounded me, said was, "Be quiet. Pay attention. I am here."

So I left my work and went to sit at the other window, first straight-backed and breathing to a count, then simply relaxing and waiting. Nothing "happened" in any ordinary sense of the word, but it was a fully packed Nothing—peace and joy and rest; solitude at its richest. I sat there in the long, slowly gathering dusk until the others came back.

The image that came with that time was of the young Indian brave (I wonder what the women

did that was comparable—does history state?) who
sat alone, waiting for his totem animal to come to
him; and how I had read somewhere that the young
man who could say no to the animals who came
would in the end have the experience of seeing a
man approach; and if he then took the man for his
totem, he would be one of the Great Ones of his
tribe. As I sat, I would not have been surprised to
see animals come out from the woods one by one
toward me across the clearing, robins and bluebirds
and squirrels and raccoons, a weasel, a fisher, a deer,
(impossibly) an eagle. And at last, if I waited, the
One, *ho anthropos*, the Anthropos, the complete
human being, would come; and what then?

It all took me back to a time that in heart
and mind I've longed for many times since it
happened. It was here, too, the first summer of the
cabin. We had been very active, but on this day near
the end of our stay, Maxey had gone off to spend
the day at Ralph Ross's workshop to make the first

set of beds, and I was alone all day. It was an amazing time, pure solitude, the real thing, with joy its content—pure joy, wave on wave of it, all day long.

I thought then that the experience was tied to this place, and expected to recapture it almost at will by coming here. But of course that was not so, and I learned quickly enough not to count on it or look for it. Many events and frustrations kept coming between me and such experiences, and I learned how vulnerable to distraction I am, and how well insulated I am against them by all the details and preoccupations of ordinary life. Even so, they manage to visit me now and then, in times full of mystery.

Mystery—it is all around us, and we do not know it. But sometimes when we give it time and space, whether in deep peace or great anguish, it will come up behind us, or meet us face to face, or move within us, changing the way we see everything, and filling our hearts with joy and an upspringing of love that needs no direct object because *everything* is its object.

JOURNAL ENTRY, FEBRUARY 12, 1950

Yesterday I got a bad case of cabin fever. The
furnace had been on too long, the doors had stayed
shut too long, the windows seemed worn thin from
looking through, after all these weeks of winter. The
house was tired of me and I was tired of it. So I went
for a walk.

But it was no better outdoors. The whole
town was winter-worn too, with cracked sidewalks
and potholes in the street. Even the brook looked as
if it could use a vacuum cleaning: two inches of
sluggish, soupy water, with summer's muck and last
fall's dead leaves lying on the bottom. "This is what
the world is made of," I said to myself, "water and
dirt—mud, that's what."

Then suddenly, without my doing anything
about it at all, my eyes refocused themselves, and
instead I saw mirrored branches of trees, and behind
them blue sky and white clouds, reflections of what
was above the brook, coming out from behind all
that dinginess—a sight that, while I was looking at

the dinginess, I had been completely unaware of. It was the same spot being looked at, the same two eyes looking, but two different worlds. As long as I looked at the brook itself, it was dark; but when I looked *through* to the reflection behind, it became full of light. And all by a simple change of attention, like turning the knob on a radio, I could see now light, now dark—but never again, I noticed, one to the complete exclusion of the other, as at that first alternation.

The more often we make a time and a space for it, the more often mystery will be a presence. As it comes and goes and returns again, we begin to have a kind of interior double vision, in which we can see the dark and the light together; and both sustain us. Being aware of these visitations of mystery that come through life helps us as we look into the deep mystery of death itself; and we gain a sense of what Psalm 139 means when it says to God, "The darkness and the light are both alike to thee."

In old age the ability to sleep well may forsake us, leaving us wakeful for two or three hours in those darkest and most interminable hours of the night, say from two to five. This can be a real affliction: we toss and turn and try angrily to fall asleep again. Or it can be an opportunity, another example of the wide-open spaces of time that childhood gave us, to use as we see fit. We can take imaginary walks; we can revisit wonderful landscapes that we have seen; we can remember, step by step, events both minor and major. We can float along happily in what May Sarton calls "a good think," to fall asleep afterward and wake refreshed with new insights.

Best of all, if we have not done it before, we can begin to learn something about prayer. If we have thought about prayer at all, we have probably considered it a deliberate act,

something that we choose to do, or not. Back in
the eighteenth century, William Law, the great
English mystic, knew better: "As the heart willeth
and worketh, such, and no other, is its prayer. . . .
For this is the necessity of our nature: pray we
must, as sure as our heart is alive; and therefore
when the state of our heart is not a spirit of
prayer to God, we pray without ceasing to some,
or other, part of the creation."

Now, in those wide-open night hours, we can begin to learn what "part of the creation" we have been praying to without knowing it—riches, strength, beauty, intellect, health, or whatever. We can watch what we do so we can find out who we are. Perhaps as we do so we can enlarge and refocus our prayer, until we find, some fine night, that we are not so much praying as being prayed through, and all our own best hopes and the hopes of the world are flowing through us. Such prayer comes and goes; it is not at our bidding. But if it happens even once, perhaps that is enough. We have caught a glimpse of what prayer can be.

In old age we have already begun to
experience time differently, but there is still
another time change waiting. We have been
governed by *chronos* time, clock time, calendar
time that dictated waking and sleeping, work and
rest. Now it is *kairos* time that guides us—*kairos*,
the right time, the appropriate time, as decided
not by clocks but by the rhythm of life itself. "A
time to get, and a time to lose; a time to keep and
a time to cast away"—the famous passage from
Ecclesiastes says it well. Inner changes call for
outward ones to match.

One of the hardest of these *kairos* times
comes when an inner voice begins to ask, "Where
is the life that late we lived?" It's gone: the work,
the family, the web of social activity that filled
our middle years. Old friends have moved away
or died; we have lost them, and gained new
neighbors whom we hardly know. The house is
empty of everyone but us, except (with luck) at

Thanksgiving or Christmas. On the other hand, creeping artifaction has done its work over the years. The house may be empty of people, but it is full of an accumulation of things, and our lives are encrusted with possessions and burdened with the work they entail. The schedule of jobs that kept house and yard in order, and that we used to do so easily, now seems more and more impossible to manage. The *kairos* voice says, "It's time!"

Yes, it's time. But time for what?

The conventional wisdom of today—
accompanied by a gentle scorn for those who
decide differently—is that the old should not
segregate themselves into their own age group,
but stay on as part of the larger, intergenerational
society. Anything less is a retreat into uselessness.

Intergenerational living has its drawbacks,
however, which can be summarized and
symbolized by drawing a mental picture of a
teenager on a skateboard and an elder with a
four-pronged cane trying to travel along the same
sidewalk. The difficulties are almost entirely a
matter of tempo, and they are serious difficulties.
We find the younger generations bewilderingly
speedy in everything they do; they find us
exasperatingly slow. Life together exhausts
patience on both sides, no matter how much love
and good will we bring to the situation.

JOURNAL ENTRY, OCTOBER 10, 1994

After a summer of intergenerational living I've been moved to reread Shakespeare's *King Lear*—not as a study in good and evil, which is its most obvious theme, but as looking deeply into old age, how it looks to itself, and how it looks to the generation behind it. Shakespeare gives the extreme picture, in which the old person is arrogant and stupid (but then, we can be that!) and the young ones are either totally rejecting and critical, as Regan and Goneril are, or totally accepting and loving, as Cordelia is. At the end Lear becomes simple and loving. It's all pure evil and pure good in the play; but in real life the psychological tangles within the individuals and between the generations are seldom that. It's a jumble, it's no one's fault, it's everyone's fault, it's existential. Younger and older don't mix easily at close quarters.

Everyone involved needs a certain amount of distance; and the old in particular need dignity and distance and privacy conferred upon them before they can show forth what lies beyond the indignities of old age—the wisdom, deliberateness, gentleness, and (with luck) peace that age can offer us and that we can give to others. If we feel at ease, we can open up like flowers; if not, our powers dry up within us, and we become all that the negative eye sees in us: confused, disorganized, stupidly slow and repetitive, to be fled from.

Some of these generational tensions can be directly dealt with. One mother-daughter pair I know took the time, after a summer of intergenerational frustrations, for a week-long trip together, during which they made a conscious effort to focus on each other, enjoy each other, and think together about what it is like to grow older (something that, after all, both of them were doing)—so that the inevitable difficulties turned from tensions into joint problem-solving exercises that they both found themselves enjoying. It was a time of pleasure and discovery, one whose good effects far outlasted the trip.

But in the long run, and for everyday life, most of all we need one another, we elders. We need to be together. We need others like us with whom we can laugh at our unreliable memories and collect jokes about our failing powers. We need to create communities in which we can be ourselves, in which we can all be in it together, sustaining one another, and finding a richness and quality of life that we did not know would be possible at our age. "The old are younger in one another's company," Gabriel García Márquez says, and as we live together we find that he is right.

A poem by Evelyn Bayless says it well,
describing the new life in a community of elders:

COMING HOME

Old friends or new, we meet in pilgrimage
here, on this tree-crowned hill of sun and shade,
our former years soft-folded on the shelf,
our memoirs stored in folders in the shed.
We seldom list past honors, children's names,
the triumphs or the tragedies we've known;
the deeper mystery is still ahead.
We try to compass it in different ways:
in sharing books that give our thoughts more room,
in correspondence to support a cause,
in tending gardens, mindful of our Earth's
green woods and pastures now in jeopardy,
in laughter, like two waves approaching shore
that meet and crest in sudden glad surprise,
in simple acts of service—daily bread—
and in awareness of the gift of life.

Supporting and encouraging one another, living at our own tempo, we can gather together the strength we need to relate to younger relatives and friends, to reach out into the larger community in our own ways, with dignity. We can stop being a problem—because we have acted together to solve it—and begin to bring into today's crises and needs some of the wisdom, patience, and long-term perspective of our years. One old woman said, "Do not deprive me of my old age; I have earned it," and we too can begin to enjoy and use what we have earned, as we spend time together.

Time together can take many forms: small groups that meet regularly for mutual support; days spent at elder centers; retirement communities; continuing care communities that will carry us all the way through the rest of our lives, providing a sustaining environment all the way. The only complaint to be made about these last is that they are available only to those foresighted enough or prosperous enough to afford them. Perhaps the day will come when they are available to everyone; but meanwhile, for those who can consider them:

JOURNAL ENTRY, APRIL 6, 1995

It's strange how sometimes life will provide the answers before you have managed to figure out the questions. In the years that I've been living at Kendal I've often wondered what makes it such an especially satisfying place to live in. And I've come to realize that two apparently minor questions can sum up the community attitudes that have had the most to do with creating the atmosphere that I like.

The first question is, "Are wheelchairs allowed in the dining room?" The answer is no in some retirement homes. Why? I suppose because of a laudable wish to have the prevailing atmosphere emphasize vigorous, healthy old age. But I think that there could be another wish that is even more laudable—to surmount rather than hide away the inevitable declines and disabilities that age will bring, more often than not—to let the wheelchairs come in. Here at Kendal the answer to that question is yes. The wheelchairs come into the dining room and go everywhere else they want to, and we see the

courage that so often accompanies disability. What is more, we have a chance to meet the many alert and interesting people who ride in them. What is still more—my time may come! And I want to be able to enjoy the full life of the community as long as I possibly can.

The second question is, "Do you have a general activities director for the residential group?" The answer is yes in many retirement homes, and it comes of a laudable wish to keep life moving along in as many interesting ways as possible. Here the answer is no, on the theory that we elders need to do what we want to do and not do what we don't want to do—and most of all, we need to make those decisions ourselves. This decision creates a place where nothing happens unless the residents initiate it. . . . And if elders are left to their own creative selves, it is amazing what they will initiate, and carry on, and enjoy together.

Other places that answer these two questions differently may be fine; but those are the answers for me, and this is the place for me.

However much it seems the right thing to do and the right time for doing it, the decision to move along into a new life pattern brings a hard time for us when we must leave the familiar setting and all the past that we have lived with and loved for so many years. It is a real wrench; but it brings another of the gifts of old age, the chance to say goodbye—a long, deep, fully conscious farewell.

JOURNAL ENTRY, JULY 2, 1988

The flow of time has taken a lot with it, and makes me feel as if I had come a long way along the stream, past many landmarks. I despair of ever being able to describe this spring.

Objectively it consisted of dividing up possessions, deciding what to keep, passing on the rest to children, grandchildren, friends. Toward the end we found ourselves saying "Take it! Take it!" to anyone who showed the faintest interest in any of our possessions.

It consisted of seeing the house gradually stripped down to its elegant bones, and saying thank you and goodbye to all its sheltering gifts of the past.

It consisted of having all the children, available grandchildren, and interested friends visit for their last times in that much-loved place.

It consisted of living through the last, hectic, exhausting days in a bad heat wave, drowning in the

scent of honeysuckle, which is growing all over the neglected yard.

And subjectively—

—finding tears near the surface at all kinds of unexpected times. At first I assumed that they were tears of sadness, but they weren't. They were tears that came from being emotionally moved, all day, every day, by how much we loved and appreciated what we had been lucky enough to have, and give, and share, and shelter, in that wonderful Noah's Ark of a place, in that pleasant town.

—being moved and also being awed at the strong sense of what a human life is; how we come, and we go, and others take our place in the stream of life. I felt as if I were standing beside a great ocean; or looking down a deep well; or looking up into space. "Mystery" was the word that kept coming to mind.

—and with it all the sense of doing our own

closure, and being glad we were doing it, and glad that we were making way for those others in the stream.

We had our day;/And look, a new one starts.

Well—I will never do this experience justice. But I'll keep on trying.

Paradoxically, the more we have allowed ourselves to love fully and freely a place or a person or a way of life, the more fully and freely we can leave it.

JOURNAL ENTRY, FEBRUARY 8, 1988, COPYING PART OF A LETTER TO A FRIEND:

I had some philosophical thoughts yesterday, one of which was in connection with what you said about not letting yourself be too fond of your house because you were going to have to leave it soon. My theory—and it does seem to work, at least where I'm concerned, is that with things and places, and possibly with people too, it's easier to let them go when you must, if you have let yourself love them, than if you've held back. There's a sense of fulfillment, of life having been fully experienced, that makes letting go be part of the fulfillment itself.

I'm finding this lengthy process of saying goodbye to this much-loved house and to our life here an extremely good one. A whole past unrolls as we sort old papers and daybooks, and events take on a perspective and clarity that they didn't have while they were unrolling themselves in an endless present.

Maybe the general truth is that *any* process, not held back from, is fulfilling and beautiful. I hope I can remember that when I am dying.

For that is where our process is taking us, to death; and in old age we live in daily awareness of that fact. Daily awareness—or daily avoidance. Avoidance is the standard modern pattern, one which we have absorbed all these years unconsciously from our culture. Now is our time, and our opportunity, to unlearn that pattern, to exchange it for a larger one that includes a larger portion of human reality.

JOURNAL ENTRY, JULY 27, 1993

Several thoughts have come together in the past few weeks: a sentence from *Borrowed Time,* an AIDS novel by Paul Monette, in which he comments that the experience of gays can be paralleled in the modern world only by that of eighty-year-olds who see their friends dying around them right and left, and know that their time too is short. And the experience in writing our book that Lynn and I have been having during these past eight years of living intimately in our thoughts with nineteenth-century people to whom death was always close, and whose lives were, in the main, short. And of course my own situation at eighty-three, conscious that I walk an ever narrowing path along a cliffside and can, with any accident inner or outer, fall off.

Anyhow, what it all added up to, the other night, in the bedroom/cell at Adelynrood, was lying

awake, running the first verse of *Abide With Me*
through my mind as part—at least—of a perfect
statement:

> *Abide with me: fast falls the eventide;*
> *The darkness deepens; Lord, with me abide:*
> *When other helpers fail and comforts flee,*
> *Help of the helpless, O abide with me.*

That was fine, but there was more that I needed: a verse ending "O thou who changest not, abide with me"—and I couldn't remember it. So in the morning I checked out the 1982 hymnal; and there was no such verse in the hymn there. So, when we got back from Adelynrood, Elsa and I checked out the 1940 hymnal, and there it was, though marked with an asterisk, which means "May be omitted"—and just as satisfying to my sense of how things are now with me as I thought it would be:

> *Swift to its close ebbs out life's little day,*
> *Earth's joys grow dim, its glories pass away,*
> *Change and decay in all around I see;*
> *O thou who changest not, abide with me.*

What is it with us moderns? We are more emancipated from the constant threat of death than any human beings at any time in our history; and yet we are more afraid of looking it in the face, of having it mentioned, even. We live each day as if we were going to live forever, and we are much the worse for it.

We need the concept of death, of "life's little day." We need it badly, for only it can give us a valid perspective. Realizing fully that we are all human, all in this together, all surrounded by change and decay, we can begin to feel compassion for ourselves and for one another. Realizing fully that we are all mortal will give us back the present, the true moment-by-moment Eternal Now, in exchange for the modern, digital-watch present familiar to us, that is merely a fast track from present to future, and that as we live it seems to have no end.

The concept of death can set us free— free to live fully in our time, free to be human beings again at last, aware of our end and of the measure of our days.

Life in old age will teach us all this, for it will inevitably take us into the valley of death, as illness takes us a little way along it ourselves, or as we travel along it with another person. The question is what we are willing to learn from these experiences. Undeniably they have their painful, frightening side, as death presents its terrifying face to us. But behind that, perhaps we can begin to see death smiling at us, as these shorter journeys bring us closer to the longer one of our own mortality.

JOURNAL ENTRY, FEBRUARY 23, 1994

"An ounce of experience can outweigh a whole pound of theory." I don't know where that quotation came from, but it's true. Every time I write persuasively and eloquently about something that I haven't experienced fully, life pulls me up short. Like death, for instance. I've written and talked about that a bit, but it was all theory. When a friend exclaimed as she lay dying, "I want to be free," I took it as simply an end-life statement of her lifelong pattern of independence. But now I hear it differently, now that I've looked into the abyss that opened up during those days in the infirmary when I was having my first ever attack of bronchial asthma, and had to work hard for every breath day and night. Now I think she was saying, "Let me go!" Or, like the eighteenth-century Quaker whom Teresina Havens quoted when she was dying, "Do not seek to hold me, for I am wound into largeness." Or like stepmother Helen, at ninety-five, saying to herself

when she thought no one was listening, "I wish I could just go off into the woods and die."

The abyss that I looked into, and that I think they did too, was/is that it can be such a *labor* to die. The body insists on having the last word; it keeps struggling for life; and life insists on continuing to the last possible moment. The process can be very hard; I found that out during the time when I was laboring to breathe every breath I drew.

Shakespeare says: "Men must endure/Their going hence, even as their coming hither."

Yes! I learned that during these past weeks. It's a travail, like the birth process. But I hope, and think, that a freedom, a lightness of being, follows this labor, this travail. Then we wind into largeness and all our work is ended. Perhaps death is the last and greatest gift of age.

An observable moving into greater
distance is part of the development of the very
old; it seems to take them longer to come back
from where they are—whatever mysterious inner
distance—to answer questions or take part in
conversations. A doctor friend of mine held the
conviction that, even where the inner distance is
so great that the personality appears to be absent,
there can be important soul-work going on. She
used to tell the story of a classically difficult
woman, an artist at keeping everyone stirred up,
who went off into a months-long unresponsive
silence, eyes closed. At the end of the time she
opened her eyes, said, "I will try to live a better
life," and died. We cannot presume to know all
that is going on interiorly during these last
stages, but we can at least have the humility to
reflect that what we can see may not be
everything that is happening.

Modern life does not give us the

experiences that might enlarge our vision.
Because of our prevailing avoidance of death, we
tend to isolate the dying. As they start off on
their long journey, we often leave them to lie
alone in hospitals and nursing homes. Or if we do
push ourselves into visiting them, we feel shy,
and think that there is nothing we can do or say.
It hardly occurs to us that the living can have
anything to say to the dying, or that the dying
have anything to communicate to the living. So
we stand helplessly at the foot of the bed for a
few minutes and then retreat to make fruitless
small-talk inquiries of the nurse in charge. We
think that the dying are beyond our reach as they
lie there, unable to speak or respond in any way,
but we are wrong. They can still hear what is said
to them, even in what seems like deep
unconsciousness; they can still be aware of touch.

One of my great and lasting regrets in life stems from my ignorance of these facts. I was sitting with a dying friend far beyond human contact (or so I thought), with instructions to see that she did not, in her restless moving, tear out her intravenous tube. She began to stir, and I went over to the bed and took her hand to keep her arm still. As I took it and said my name, she turned eagerly toward me and her face brightened. That, if I had been smart enough to know it, was my cue to take a seat by the bed, and hold her hand, and perhaps talk to her a little. But I was a child of my time, blind and stupid. I settled her arm down again, as instructed, and returned to my seat a safe and detached ten feet away, across the room.

It used to be different. People would die at home, surrounded by their families. It was a terrible time for everyone, with agonizing and exhausting days and nights of physical care of a

quality that was probably appalling by any modern standards; but with all our gains we have lost something essential—the privilege of saying a close and conscious farewell to the people we love, and of being with them to the end.

Nowadays all that is so much a lost art that we have no awareness that the dying need us to go as far as we can with them on their journey. One old woman, when she was dying and a well-meaning visitor sat discreetly at a distance and talked about higher things, protested, "But that's not what I need! What I want right now is human contact and lots of it." The dying need us to stay with them: just being there, for the most part, but always ready to touch them, talk, and even sing to them. They need us to love them. Given that kind of loving support, as hospice workers often testify, dying can be a good, sometimes even a glorious experience. Irene Claremont de Castillejo, in the chapter of *Knowing Woman* (C. Jung Foundation, 1973) called "What Is the Meaning of Love?" writes, on page 122, "Love and death are strangely kin. . . . We need love to be able to die serenely."

And so the soul moves into its long journey, in which, as one Eastern sage said, there is no need for it to go anywhere—paradox again—and we can follow only in imagination.

My own imagining, when I have been privileged to walk partway through the valley of death with someone, is that we walk together down a gently sloping hillside to a stream. At the stream, they cross and I pause, watching while they go up a slope on the other side, disappearing into a mist. My doctor friend, who has sat by many a deathbed and gone much farther along the journey than I, reported that in nearly every instance, as she watched—and she had learned to watch closely—she would see, at the moment of death, a fleeting expression of incredulous joy cross the face of the dying one, as if something were happening that exceeded all dreams and all hopes and all promises.

Having seen this, she wrote, near the end of her own life, "Never having died, I believe it is an experience I don't want to miss; I want to experience dying in its entirety, if circumstances permit."

We do not know. We cannot know. But meanwhile we can watch what we do so we can find out who we are before we come to the end of the long day that is our life.

For that day we have a guide in a prayer, a fourth-century prayer of St. Ambrose:

May the day go by joyously:
In the morning of purity,
In the high noon of faith,
And without nightfall upon the spirit.

So let us close—with luck and good management—without nightfall upon our spirit, capable as it is of great things clear to the end.

While we have the light,
let us walk in the light.
In God's light, let us see light.
Amen.

SUGGESTED READING

This list is firmly based on personal choice and includes only books that I have found absorbing and inspiring upon first and second and sometimes third or more readings. These are not books *about* aging, but rather books written from within the experience either of the aged or of those who love them—or from within the experience as seen with artistic imagination. Some of them are fiction, some are journals, some are plays or poetry.

All Passion Spent by V. Sackville-West. Originally published in 1931, but reprinted since. A fine novel about the last year in the life of an old woman. Dramatized a few years ago on *Masterpiece Theatre*.

Memory Board by Jane Rule, Naiad Press, 1987. Another fine novel about two aging women, one of whom is failing mentally, the other physically, the central theme of which is the life which they and their friends build around the almost complete memory loss of one of them.

The Names of the Mountains by Reeve Lindbergh, Simon & Schuster,

1992. A loving portrait of an old woman with increasing memory loss, and of how the family that surrounds her responds to it. Beautifully written, and deftly including the kind of humorous incidents that can occur within the sorrows of such a time.

Crossing to Safety by Wallace Stegner, Penguin Books, 1988. An absorbing novel by one of our best modern novelists, dealing with the pleasures, problems, and changes in a four-way friendship over a period of fifty years, as told by one of the friends: a good example of the perspective—the insights and the wisdom—that can come from a thoughtful look at the past.

Ulysses by Alfred Tennyson. Since most of the previous titles have dealt with aging in women's experience, it is good to have this poem giving a brief and brilliant picture of what aging can mean to a man.

King Lear, Hamlet, and *The Tempest* by William Shakespeare. More about aging as experienced by men—the loss of perspective and power, the disastrous folly and the saving wisdom that can come with age.

Emma, Persuasion, and *Pride and Prejudice* by Jane Austen. These are cautionary pictures—the first, in Mr. Woodhouse, of a querulous old man and his effect on the group around him; the second, in Sir Walter Elliott, of a man growing old who will not stop living as if he were young and stylish, and rich. The third offers a balancing picture, in Mrs. Bennet, of an aging woman who never grew up in the first place and refuses to grow up now.

Old Age: Journey into Simplicity by Helen Luke, Parabola Books,

1987. An examination of the wisdom that growing old can offer, as seen through portions of *The Odyssey, King Lear, The Tempest,* and T. S. Eliot's *Little Gidding.*

Look Me in the Eye by Barbara Macdonald with Cynthia Rich, Spinsters Ink, San Francisco, 1982. Essays on the experience of becoming invisible and inaudible, among other aspects of aging.

The Measure of My Days by Florida Scott-Maxwell, Knopf. Originally published in 1968, but often reprinted. A meditative, inward look at aging, written in a loose journal form in the author's eighties.

Aging and *Reaching Out,* both by Henri Nouwen, Doubleday, 1976. *Reaching Out,* while not primarily about aging, offers valuable insight on loneliness and solitude and how to move from one state into the other.

The Divine Milieu by Pierre Teilhard de Chardin. The concept of "diminishment," as treated in this book, can be very helpful in thinking about aging.

And, of course, the Bible. Scripture offers several passages that are helpful in contemplating aging, notably in the beautiful imagery of Ecclesiastes, Chapter 12, and the passage on time, 3:1–8. Helpful verses are scattered all through the Psalms, with numbers 23, 46, and 139 as strengtheners at any and all times.

ACKNOWLEDGMENTS

Thanks are due and gladly given to many people for helping this book to come out of its hiding place in a series of notebooks:

First of all to Stephen Morrison, without whom it would never be in print at all.

Then to my agent Liv Blumer, who shepherded the material into its final form, and has been a constant joy to work with and claim as a friend.

To Eric Major, Doubleday Editor, for the vision with which he has brought the material into its final form and setting.

And to Elizabeth D. Walter, of Doubleday, who saved me from an unfortunate tendency to remember quotations inaccurately, and otherwise kept me out of trouble along the way.

And earlier, to Rebecca Kratz Mays, Editor of Pendle Hill Publications, for publishing in 1993 a short version of this material as the pamphlet "Without Nightfall Upon the Spirit."

Earliest of all, to the Rev. Charlene Fulton, who

cornered me into giving the talk on aging at St. Andrew's Church in Yardley, Pennsylvania that began the whole process of putting my thoughts on the subject into some kind of order.

Thanks, too, to Morris West for his gracious preface.

And to Donald Hall and Graywolf Press for allowing me to quote the poem by Jane Kenyon, "Let Evening Come," which gives its title to the text. And to Harcourt Brace for the use of quotations from T. S. Eliot's *Ash Wednesday* and *Four Quartets.*

To Evelyn Bayless for the use of her poem "Coming Home."

To my husband, Maxey, for many years of gentle, encouraging loving kindness.

And finally, I owe more thanks than I can express to the many individuals, dead and alive, ancient and modern, who have contributed, in their writings and coversations and ways of life, to my thinking on this subject over many years.